Your Baby's Baptism

in the Anglican Church

Beginning a wonderful journey of love

Alison Evans

**kevin
mayhew**

First published in Great Britain in 2009 by Kevin Mayhew Ltd
Buxhall, Stowmarket, Suffolk IP14 3BW
Tel: +44 (0) 1449 737978 Fax: +44 (0) 1449 737834
E-mail: info@kevinmayhewltd.com

www.kevinmayhew.com

9 8 7 6

ISBN 978 0 86209 801 8
Catalogue No. 1425050

Cover design by Rob Mortonson
Typeset by Sarah Ricks
© Images used under licence from Shutterstock Inc.

Printed and bound in Great Britain

Baptism is a deep and truly wonderful gift.

Deciding to have your child baptised is an occasion for joy and celebration, but it must also be undertaken seriously and thoughtfully. As you read through this booklet, we hope it will help you to understand more deeply what baptism is, what it means for your child and your responsibilities as their parent or guardian. We also hope it will help you to enjoy and cherish the baptism of your child, as they embark on their journey with God, with guidance from you and their godparents.

Why baptism?

Parents often find that having a child is a more profound experience than they've ever had before.

- This leads some to seek baptism as they start to think about what life is really about.

- For others it confirms the belief in God they already had.

- Many more are seeking answers to questions about their own life and the life of their child.

Baptism opens up the realisation that we can only begin to make sense of our lives when we allow God in. Your child will inevitably grow up and draw their own conclusions, but baptism will at least set them off in the right direction.

The birth of a child is of course a happy and life-changing occasion, but too often people think that baptism is just part of a sequence of events involved in having a baby, choosing to get their child baptised because 'that's what you do'. Although baptism is a reason to celebrate, it is not just an excuse for a party! If you are not ready to make the promises of baptism, there is a special service of Thanksgiving in which you can thank God for the life of your child. Ask your priest about this.

Not just an excuse for a party!

Living in God's love

Baptism is about offering ourselves to Christ and entering into a relationship of love with God. This doesn't mean we must forget who we are; each of us is an individual with our own personality, strengths and weaknesses. What it does mean is that we can have the courage and confidence to turn our backs on darkness, living our lives in the light of Christ.

Each of us is an individual with our own personality, strengths and weaknesses

We can know for sure that whatever happens in our lives, we are totally and completely loved by God and that whatever we ask in his name, we will receive if we live in Christ (John 15:7).

We are totally and completely loved by God

God wants to free us so we can fully be who he made us to be. He wants us to enjoy and embrace our lives, but the only way we can truly do that is to live in his love. Baptism is God's gift to us, but it is also our way to tell him we accept his love and wish to live in his light.

God wants to free us so we can fully be who he made us to be

What is baptism?

A gift from God

Baptism is first and foremost a gift from God.

At the heart of the Christian faith is the belief that although it is impossible for us to deserve God's love and forgiveness through our own doing, we don't have to worry because God sent his only son into the world to die in our place. Jesus took all of our sins upon himself, he received our punishment for us, and because of this we have been forgiven for all our wrongdoings.

We have been forgiven for all our wrongdoings

This is not an excuse to behave badly and never take responsibility for our actions, rather it is an invitation to live a good life with Christ that is full of peace and joy. Through his death and Resurrection, Christ showed us that we too can receive eternal life with God.

Live a good life with Christ that is full of peace and joy

God the Father declared Jesus as his Son when he was baptised in the River Jordan (Matthew 3:17). We too publicly enter into God's family through our own baptism. The Church encourages baptism to take place in the main Sunday worship, so that the whole Church family can welcome their new member. Although private baptism is in many ways a contradiction in terms, it is not disallowed. This is something you can discuss with your priest.

Christians united

When we are baptised, we become part of one 'body'. This means we become part of the Church, which is God's 'body'. Baptism unites us with Christians all over the world, from the past, present and future; we have a connection with them that cannot be broken. We each shine God's love and light into the world through our gifts and abilities, contributing in our own unique way to the overall Church family. We also have a responsibility to recognise the gifts of our Christian brothers and sisters and love them as our family, sharing in their joy and heartache, failure and success (1 Corinthians 12:13–26).

Baptism unites us with Christians all over the world, from the past, present and future

Promises made

There are certain promises that we each have to make when we are baptised. As your baby cannot make these for themselves you as the parents, along with the godparents, make them on their behalf.

Some important questions to ask yourself when choosing godparents are:

- Will they make friends with my child?

- Will they help my child to know the Lord Jesus and grow in their Christian faith?

- Will they encourage my child to be part of the Church family?

- Will they pray for my child?

A child's attitude to God is mostly shaped by their parents in their early years, and it is your responsibility to ensure your child grows spiritually as well as mentally and physically.

Nurture their life in Christ

In having your child baptised you are formally declaring that you think their spirituality is important and that you intend to nurture their life in Christ.

The role of godparents

Usually a child will have godparents when they are baptised. The rules will depend on which part of the Anglican Church you belong to but, for example, the Church of England says you must have at least three godparents and two must be the same sex as the baby.

Godparents don't have to be family members, but you must ensure you choose people who you trust and who will be part of your baby's life. Don't just choose people who you happen to be friendly with at the moment.

Godparents have a duty

- to help your child get to know God

- to support them

- to pray for them

- to love them.

They are not just there to give good presents! Godparents need to have been baptised themselves.

The service

The form of the service will vary according to your Church. It will also depend on whether the baptism is part of an informal family service or part of the Eucharist.

There are core elements that all baptism services have, including:

- expressing a desire to be baptised, which you and the godparents will do on your child's behalf

- professing the Christian faith

- a prayer for those baptised that they may know God's kingdom

- a declaration of the responsibility of parents and godparents to bring the child up in Christ

- a welcome into the Church family.

Ask your priest for a copy of the service in which your child's baptism will take place, including everything that you and the godparents will have to say. Your priest will be more than happy to run through this with you as part of the baptism preparation.

Take a copy home with you so that you have time to think about what it is you are going to promise and what that means for you and your baby.

On the day the congregation will say some of the words with you, to support you and show that they welcome your child into the Church family.

Don't be afraid to talk to your priest about any concerns you have or anything you're unsure about. Baptism is not a test and the priest is not going to judge you, they are there to help you get ready for the baptism and talk through anything that is on your mind.

Baptism is not a test and the priest is not going to judge you

Don't worry if your baby starts to cry when they are being baptised. This happens a lot and is generally a sign of shock because they have suddenly been immersed in water rather than being a sign of disagreement. There is no need to feel embarrassed – the priest will be used to it!

Declarations

Whichever form the baptism service takes, you will be asked to publicly announce the desire to be baptised, on your baby's behalf, rejecting sin and turning to Christ.

These are called declarations – the number and exact wording varies within the Anglican Community but, as an example, the Church of England has six set declarations.

- The first three declarations are about rejecting and repenting of all evil and sin, because in order to turn fully to Christ we need to turn our backs on all the things that go against his love. To 'repent' means to 'think again' and this means admitting when we have fallen short of God's standards and behaved in ways that have spoiled our relationship with him and with other people.

Priest	Do you reject the devil and all rebellion against God?
Reply	I reject them.
Priest	Do you renounce the deceit and corruption of evil?
Reply	I renounce them.
Priest	Do you repent of the sins that separate us from God and neighbour?
Reply	I repent of them.

- The next three declarations are about asking Christ for his forgiveness, turning to him as the only one who can save us. We submit to him as our Lord and declare that he is the way, the truth and the life.

Priest	Do you turn to Christ as Saviour?
Reply	I turn to Christ.
Priest	Do you submit to Christ as Lord?
Reply	I submit to Christ.
Priest	Do you come to Christ, the way, the truth and the life?
Reply	I come to Christ.

Symbols

There are many important symbols within the baptism service.

Sign of the cross

After the declarations the priest will make the sign of the cross on your baby's forehead. This is the sign of Christ, confirming that your child belongs to Christ.

Water

Water in baptism is a sign that we are washed free of our sins and can begin our new life with Christ. First the priest will say some prayers over the water; not to turn it into 'magical' water, but to ask God to bless the water with his love which he is about to pour into your child's life. The priest will then either dip your child into the water, or pour it over their head saying:

> *(Name)*, I baptise you
> in the name of the Father,
> and of the Son,
> and of the Holy Spirit.
> Amen.

Oil

In some churches, after the baptism with water, the priest may anoint your child with oil as a sign of the outpouring of the Holy Spirit.

Your baby is now part of the Church family

The welcome

The congregation will say some formal words of welcome to joyfully acknowledge that your baby is now part of the Church family.

Candles

At the end of the baptism the priest will give you a lighted candle. This is so you and your child can remember this special commitment you have made. It is also a symbol of Christ himself, that he is the Light of the World and that he gives us his light in which we can walk for the rest of our lives.

What baptism is not

Baptism is not a passport to heaven

It is not true that only those who are baptised can go to heaven; God loves each and every one of us equally. We cannot fool God; he knows exactly what is going on in our hearts and minds so, although baptism is open to everyone, it should not be undertaken simply to score points 'upstairs'.

God loves each and every one of us equally

Baptism does not give a child a name

This is done when the child's birth is registered with the appropriate register office.

Life after baptism

Baptism is the beginning of the journey, not the end.

With baptism we become part of God's family and a member of the worldwide Christian community. Through baptism we know that Christ is walking beside us and guiding us, but this doesn't mean that life will always be a barrel of laughs. We will still have bad days and difficult times, because that is part of life. The important thing to remember is to lean on God during those times; they are when we need him most.

Through baptism we know that Christ is walking beside us and guiding us during the difficult times

God has promised to be with us in every part of our lives so you don't have to wait until the next church service to know he is with you.

Jesus will never be too busy for you

It's easy to put 'religion' off until it's more convenient – when the children are older, when they have started school, when they have finished school, when they have left home. It's even easier to never get round to it. Remember that wherever you are, however you feel, Jesus is there beside you. No matter how many times you are too busy for him, he will never be too busy for you.

Demonstrate your Christian faith in the way you live and the attitudes you hold

As your baby grows up, you will encourage them to live a good life and set them a good example. Moral and ethical standards are generally based on a belief system, and children need to understand this belief if they are to live by it. This is something they will learn from you, so it's vital that you demonstrate your Christian faith in the way you live and the attitudes you hold.

Encourage your child to embrace the wonderful world that God has created for us

One of the best ways to do this is to make the most of your life.

- Encourage your child to embrace the wonderful world that God has created for us and help them to find their place in it.

- Give them whatever opportunity you can to discover and develop their God-given gifts and talents.

- Don't try and force them into a rigid pattern so they become frustrated, instead help them grow mentally and emotionally so they also learn to value other people's gifts and contributions to our world.

- In the same way, help them to grow spiritually and know the love of God.

Getting to know God should be a joy rather than a burden. You can read Bible stories as a family but allow your child to enjoy these stories, talking to them about what they might mean and allowing them the freedom to grow into their own relationship with God.

Just say what is in your heart

Praying together is so important, especially in worrying times. There is no need to feel embarrassed about doing this, because Jesus is there with you anyway: just say what is in your heart.

Don't forget that you also belong to the Church, and you can lean on your Church family for support whenever you need it.

You can lean on your Church family for support

Attending church can help all of the family to grow spiritually. It also means you are letting God be a part of your life, and this will give you strength and confidence to help you through the good times and bad times for the rest of your life.

Frequently asked questions

What is the difference between baptism and christening?

There is no difference, they are just different names for the same thing. To be christened means to be 'Christed' or to 'become Christ's'. In the Bible it is always called baptism. The word baptism originates from a Greek word that in English means 'to immerse'.

What's the point of godparents?

Godparents have a duty to help your child get to know God. They don't have to be family members, but they should be people who you trust and who will take their responsibility seriously. Godparents need to have been baptised themselves.

Can I have my baby baptised if I'm not a regular churchgoer?

Yes you can. Baptism is open to everybody because God loves everybody. Your priest can't force you to attend church, but it is their responsibility to ensure you fully understand what baptism is. Talk to them about what you believe and what you want for your child. There is also a Thanksgiving Service you can have for your baby if you feel you are not quite ready for baptism.

Is there an age limit on baptism?

No, you can be baptised at any age. Baptism of older children and adults is becoming increasingly common. Talk to your priest about this, but try not to force your older child into baptism if they don't want it as this can lead to resentment against the Church and God.

How much does baptism cost?

Baptism is a gift from God and so it is free. However a lot of people feel they would like to give a contribution to the church as a way of expressing thanks. Your church will normally have a collection plate and you can add your contribution to this, but only give what you can afford.

If you have any other questions about baptism, please do speak to your priest. There is no such thing as a stupid question and they will do their best to help you – that is what they are there for!

Prayers

Baptism

Thank you, Lord, for the love you give to me.
Let the water be a sign of your grace
and of my commitment to you
as I submit myself to it in faith.
Thank you for making me
a member of your body, the Church,
and grant that together
we may show your love in the world.

• •

As the falling raindrops
make the trees and flowers grow,
may the water of baptism
help this little one to blossom
in spirit, in grace and in understanding.
In the name of Jesus Christ.
Amen.

• •

Thank you, O God,
for the wonderful gift of a child.
Hold us together in your love,
and in the community of your people.
As we grow together,
may we be signs of your grace to one another.

Children learn what they live

We learn to love,
not by being told to love,
but by being loved.

• •

If your child lives with criticism,
they learn to condemn.
If your child lives with hostility,
they learn to fight.
If your child lives with ridicule,
they learn to be shy.
If your child lives with shame,
they learn to feel guilty.
If your child lives with tolerance,
they learn to be patient.
If your child lives with encouragement,
they learn confidence.
If your child lives with praise,
they learn to appreciate.
If your child lives with fairness,
they learn justice.
If your child lives with security,
they learn to have faith.
If your child lives with approval,
they learn to like themselves.
If your child lives with acceptance and friendship,
they learn to find love in the world.

Be yourself

The challenge is to be yourself
in a world that is trying
to make you like everyone else.

e. e. cummings

· ·

I asked Jesus

I asked Jesus,
'How much do you love me?'
'This much,' he answered,
and he stretched his arms out and died.

· ·

Prayer of Dedication

Lord Jesus,
I give my hands to do your work.
I give you my feet to go your way.
I give my eyes to see as you do.
I give you my tongue to speak your words.
I give you my mind that you may think in me.
I give you my spirit that you may pray in me.
Above all, I give you my heart that you may love in me.
I give you my whole self that you may grow in me,
so that it is you, Lord Jesus,
who lives and works and prays in me.

· ·

Heavenly Father

Heavenly Father,
we thank you from our hearts
for our new baby
whom you have sent into our lives
and put into our care.
We ask for grace and wisdom
as we take on the responsibility
for this new life.
May our child grow
in strength and health,
in knowledge and understanding,
and learn the joy
of walking in your ways,
through Jesus Christ our Lord.
Amen.